Mel Bay's Modern
GUITAR METHOD
GRADE 2
Expanded Edition

MW00560961

1 2 3 4 5 6 7 8 9 0

Visit us on the Web at www.melbay.com — E-mail us at email@melbay.com

The Notes on the First String

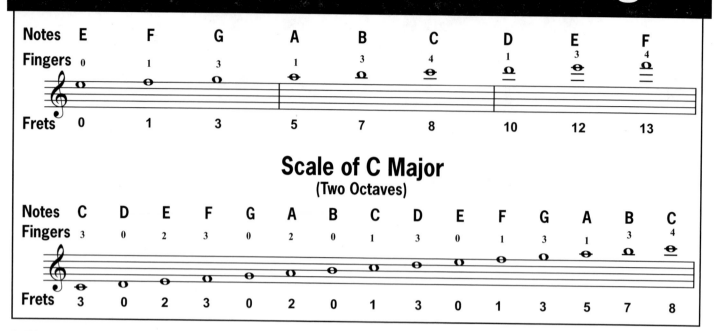

Scale of C Major
(Two Octaves)

A Rhythm Review

X – – – – – – – – – – –
Hold first finger down.

X – – – – – – – – – – –

X – – – – – – – – – – –

Accompaniment for the Above Exercises

| C | G7 | C | F | C | D7 | G7 | C |

Alternate Picking

One of the most difficult things for the student is the mastery of the alternate stroke on diatonic passages.

To promote greater speed with proper accentation, the alternate stroke should be developed.

The following study will seem difficult at first; but, by practicing slowly and placing the downstrokes on the beats followed by an upstroke, the desired result will be accomplished.

Key of C Review

Etude CD 1 #2

Picking Studies CD 1 #3

3

③ 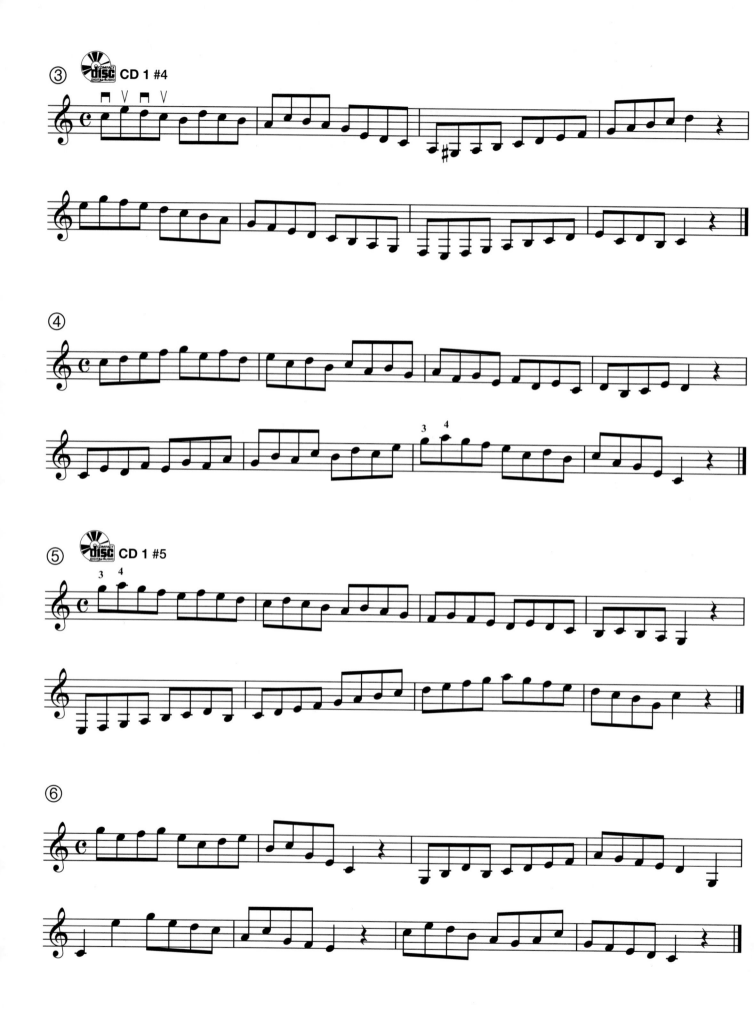 CD 1 #4

④

⑤ CD 1 #5

⑥

4

Leapfrog

Guitar Duet CD 1 #8

Allegro

Arr. by Mel Bay

Bull Durham
Swing Feeling  CD 1 #9

W.Bay

Frolic
Guitar Duet CD 1 #10

Arr. by Mel Bay

7

Frog Junction

CD 1 #11

Swing Feeling

W. Bay

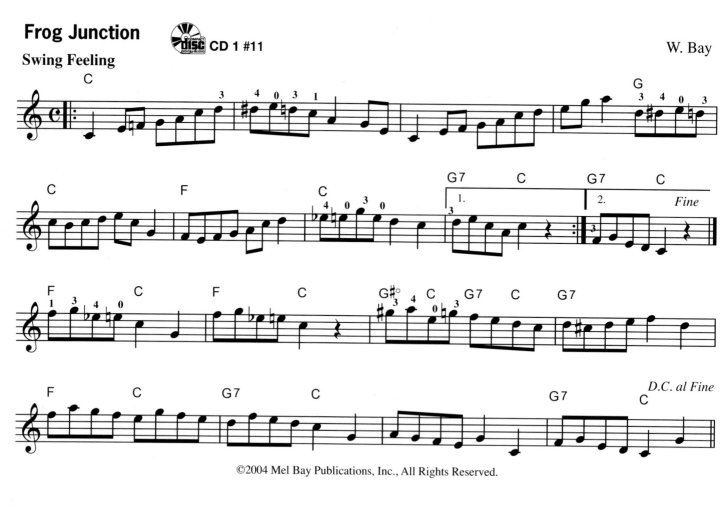

Catawissa Blues

CD 1 #12

Slowly

W. Bay

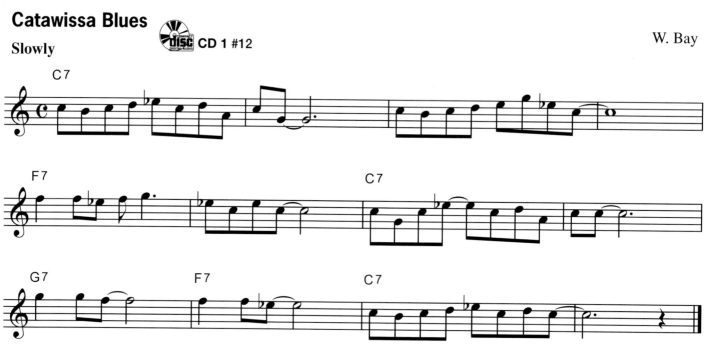

Key of A Minor Review

Picking Studies

9

Let the first note of each measure ring.

11

Prelude in C/Am
Slowy
CD 1 #19

W. Bay

C/Am Etude
Moderately
CD 1 #20

W. Bay

Old Pail

Bluegrass

W. Bay

CD 1 #21

©2004 Mel Bay Publications, Inc., All Rights Reserved.

Kuranda

Slowy

W. Bay

CD 1 #22

©2005 Mel Bay Publications, Inc., All Rights Reserved.

13

Señorita

Andante

CD 1 #23

Based on a Theme by Carcassi

Nocturne

Andante

W. Bay

CD 1 #24

Fine

D.C. al Fine

14

Valse

CD 1 #25

W. Bay

Flowing Tempo

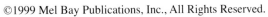
Fine

D.C. al Fine

Russian Dance

CD 1 #26

W. Bay

Allegro

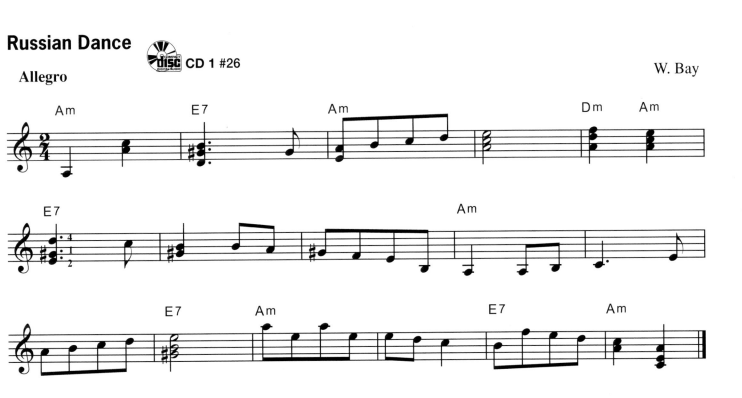

Key of G Review

Picking Studies

① CD 1 #27

②

③ CD 1 #28

④

Trekking

Lively

CD 1 #31

W. Bay

Fine

D.C. al Fine

Lavender Waltz

Slowly

CD 1 #32

W. Bay

Fine

D.C. al Fine

Accidentals are effective only in the measures in which they are found. When that measure is passed, the accidentals become void.

In the following solo, *The Guachos*, the third part is in the key of C, which explains the natural on the fifth line in the signature.

The Gauchos
Guitar Solo   CD 1 #33

Carcassi - Bay

Poinsietta   CD 1 #34

W. Bay

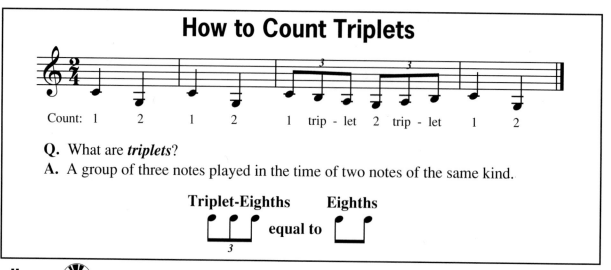

How to Count Triplets

Count: 1 2 1 2 1 trip-let 2 trip-let 1 2

Q. What are *triplets*?
A. A group of three notes played in the time of two notes of the same kind.

Triplet-Eighths **Eighths**

equal to

Tarantelle

CD 1 #35

Moderato All ⊓ stroke

Count 1 trip-let 2 trip-let 1 2

A Triple Play

Guitar Solo Moderato ⊓ V ⊓

CD 1 #36

Mel Bay

Triplet Duet

CD 1 #37

Moderato All ⊓ stroke Pupil to practice both parts.

Far From Home　CD 1 #39　　　　　　　　　　　　　　Shetland Island Reel

The Teetotaller's Reel　CD 1 #40

E Minor Review

Picking Studies

① CD 1 #41

②

③ CD 1 #42

④

Excursion

Andante

CD 1 #43

W. Bay

Fine

D.C. al Fine

Jazz Etude

Swing Feeling

CD 1 #44

W. Bay

Fine

D.C. al Fine

Forest Trail

Moderately

CD 1 #45

W. Bay

Brighton Waltz

Slowly

CD 1 #46

W. Bay

Razorback

Rhythmically

CD 1 #47

W. Bay

The Hope (Hatikvoh)

Moderately

CD 1 #48

Hebrew Song

rit.

Wade in the Water

©2000 Mel Bay Publications, Inc., All Rights Reserved.

27

The Key of F

The key of F has one flat. All B notes will be played one half step lower as shown.

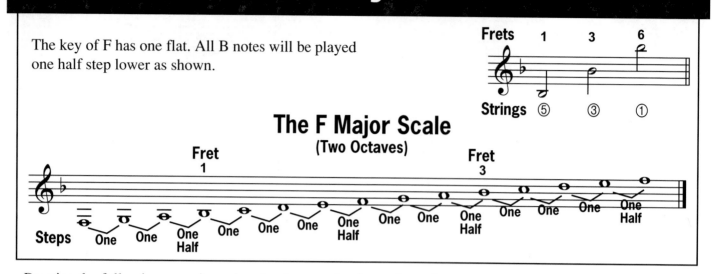

Practice the following exercise using the downstroke throughout. Later on, use the alternate stroking shown.

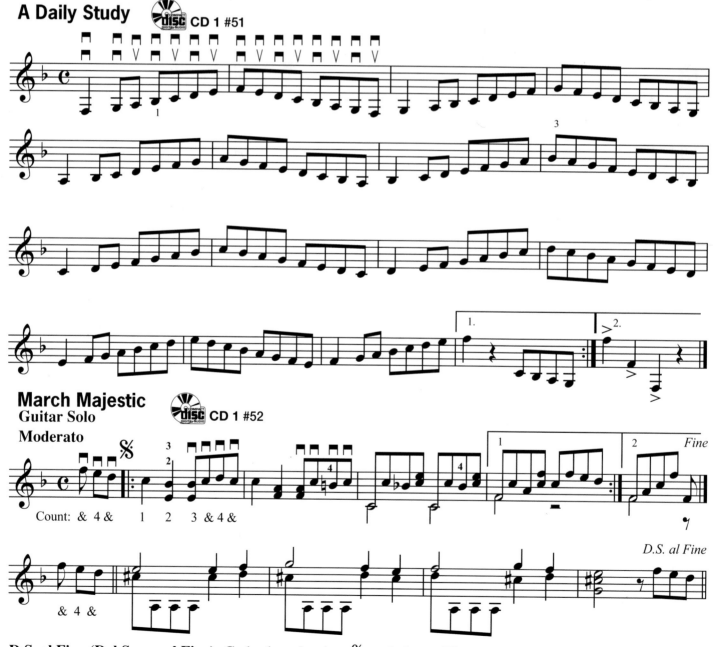

D.S. al Fine (Dal Segno al Fine): Go back to the sign 𝄋 and play to **Fine**, the end.

28

Key of F

Picking Studies

Chords in the Key of F

The three chords in the key of F are F, B flat, and C7.

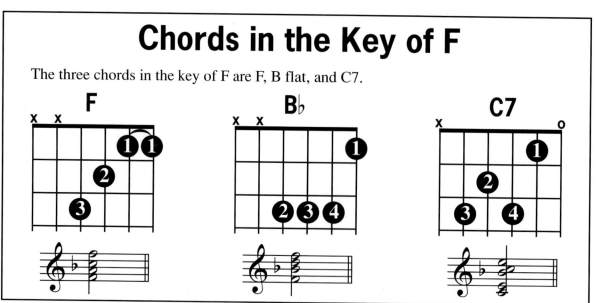

Accompaniment Styles

Common Time

Three-Four Time

Two-Four Time

Melody in F

Guitar Solo

Moderato

CD 1 #59

Rubenstein-Bay

Musical Terms

Sforzando (sfz) – Forcing the tone suddenly loud
Ad libitum (a piacere) – At the liberty of the performer
A tempo – Back to the regular tempo
Animato – Lively
Cantabile – In a singing style
Crescendo (cresc.) – Gradually grow louder

Diminuendo (dim.) – Gradually grow softer
Sostenuto – Sustained
Dolce – Sweetly
Maestoso – Majestic
Morendo – Dying or fading away
Piu mosso – Quicker

I Love Thee
Guitar Duet

CD 1 #60

Christian Hymn

Fargo

Moderato

CD 1 #61

W. Bay

Fine

D.C. al Fine

Silverheel's Shuffle

Swing Feeling

CD 1 #62

W. Bay

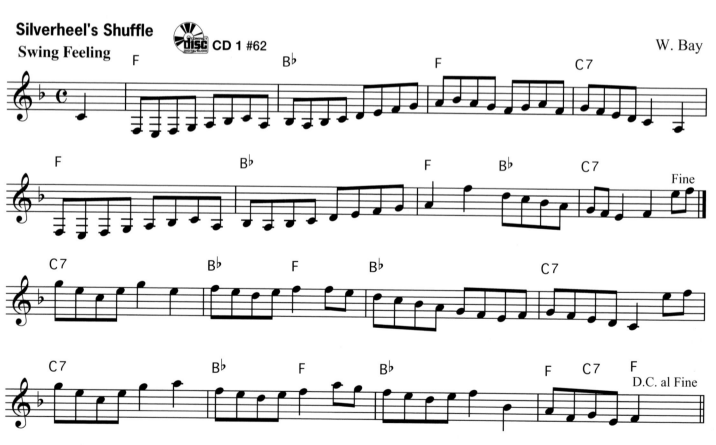

Fine

D.C. al Fine

Intervals

An **interval** is the distance between two tones or the difference in pitch between two tones when sounded.

Intervals are measured **upward** from the lower tone to the higher.

Intervals have **number** names and **type** names. For example, a 3rd could be major or minor depending upon the distance.

The staff degree occupied by the lower note and the staff degree occupied by the higher note are **both included** when determining the number name in the interval.

Below are nine intervals from C to each note in the C scale.

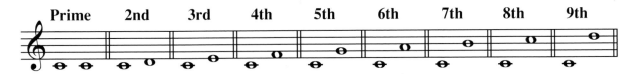

The **types** of intervals will be discussed later.

A Daily Study in F CD 1 #63

In the following solo, *The Carousel,* the second part is in the key of C.

The first line is repeated and, after the second line is played, the first line is played only once, ending at Fine. This will give the solo a total of 32 measures.

It should be practiced slowy at first and continued until a happy, spirited tempo is attained.

The Carousel CD 1 #64
Guitar Solo

D.C. al Fine

The Recital

Guitar Duet

CD 1 #65

Mazas
Arr. by Mel Bay

Moderato

Triplet Etude

All downstroke

CD 1 #66

The Happy Farmer

Guitar Solo

CD 1 #67

Robert Schumann
(Op. 68, No. 10)
Arr. by Mel Bay

Allegretto

Bubba's Bounce

Allegro, Swing Feeling

CD 1 #68

W. Bay

Soulard

Swing

CD 1 #69

W. Bay

The Key of D Minor

(Relative to F Major)

The D Minor Scales

Harmonic

Melodic

Etude in D Minor   CD 1 #70

Harmonic

Melodic

Picking Studies   CD 1 #71

①

39

41

The Chords in the Key of D Minor

The three principal chords in the key of D minor are:

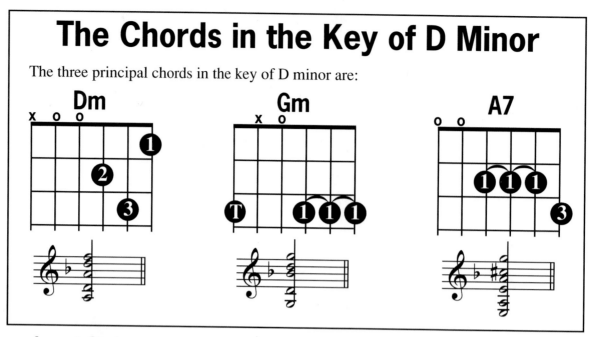

Accompaniment Styles
Common Time

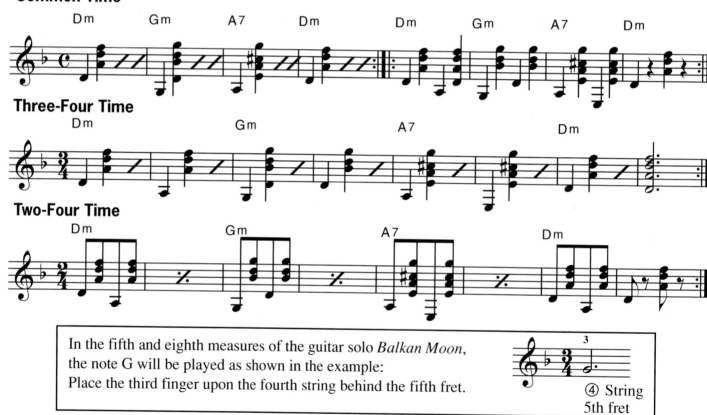

Three-Four Time

Two-Four Time

In the fifth and eighth measures of the guitar solo *Balkan Moon*, the note G will be played as shown in the example:
Place the third finger upon the fourth string behind the fifth fret.

④ String
5th fret

Balkan Moon
Guitar Solo CD 1 #76

Mel Bay

42

Finger Gymnastics

The following exercises have a two-fold purpose:

1. Training the individual fingers to perform independently of each other.
2. Acquainting the student with the technique of position playing that will be an important part of this course.

The first finger should be held down throughout these exercises.

Duet in D Minor

Guitar Duet

CD 1 #77

Mazas
Arr. by Mel Bay

* High Bb – 1st string, 6th fret

43

Andante CD 1 #78

W. Bay

Fine

D.C. al Fine

March Slav
Guitar Solo CD 1 #79

Tschaikowsky
Arr. by Mel Bay

Slow

Invention in Dm

CD 1 #80

Andante

W. Bay

Fine

D.C. al Fine

Bucharest

Swing Feeling

CD 1 #81

W. Bay

Shown below are the notes on the second string.

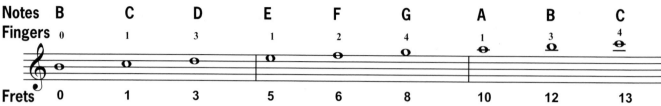

Notes	B	C	D	E	F	G	A	B	C
Fingers	0	1	3	1	2	4	1	3	4
Frets	0	1	3	5	6	8	10	12	13

Any note played upon the first string may be played upon the second string **five frets higher** than its location on the first string.

In the diagram on the right you will see the notes on the first string and, directly below, the same notes played upon the second string. This is a very good aid in remembering the notes on the second string.

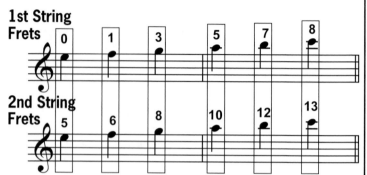

The C Scale in Thirds

The following study should be played upon the first and second strings.

The **top note will be on the first string** and the **bottom note on the second**.

To facilitate execution, it is better to let the fingers remain upon the strings as much as possible, gliding from fret to fret.

An Exercise in Thirds   CD 1 #82

Moderato

46

A Song in D Minor

CD 1 #83

Slow

Mel Bay

Swing Low Sweet Chariot

CD 1 #84

Slowly

Spiritual

Valse in Dm  CD 1 #85

W. Bay

The Rights of Man 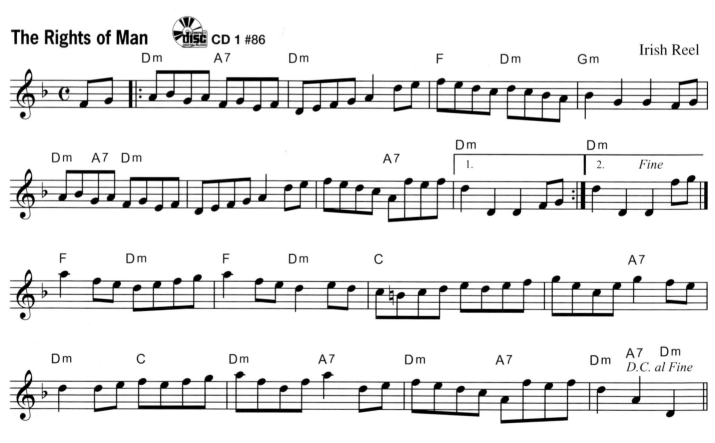 CD 1 #86

Irish Reel

The Major Chord

The major chord is formed by combining the first, third, and fifth tones of the major scale.

The first tone of the scale is known as the **root** of the chord.

The major chord may be arranged in three positions called inversions.

Thirds in the Key of F   CD 2 #1

Juanita

Guitar Solo   Moderato   CD 2 #2

Arr. by Mel Bay

49

Dolores

Andantino

CD 2 #3

Waldteufel, Op. 170
Arr. by Mel Bay

Romance

Guitar Duet

CD 2 #4

Mazas
Arr. by Mel Bay

Andante

dolce

50

Trail Ridge
Guitar Duet

CD 2 #5

Arr. Mel Bay

Manitou
Slowly

CD 2 #6

Arr. Mel Bay

Mesa Verde
Moderato

CD 2 #7

Arr. Mel Bay

Where You There?

Slowly

CD 2 #8

Spiritual

Now the Day is Over
Guitar Duet

CD 2 #9

Slowly

Hymn

52

Sonatina
Guitar Duet

CD 2 #10

Mazas
Arr. by Mel Bay

Andante

The Key of D Major

The key of D major has two sharps — F♯ and C♯.

To facilitate the fingering in the key of D major, it is necessary to move the first finger to the second fret, the second finger to the third fret, and the third finger to the fourth fret.

The D Major Scale

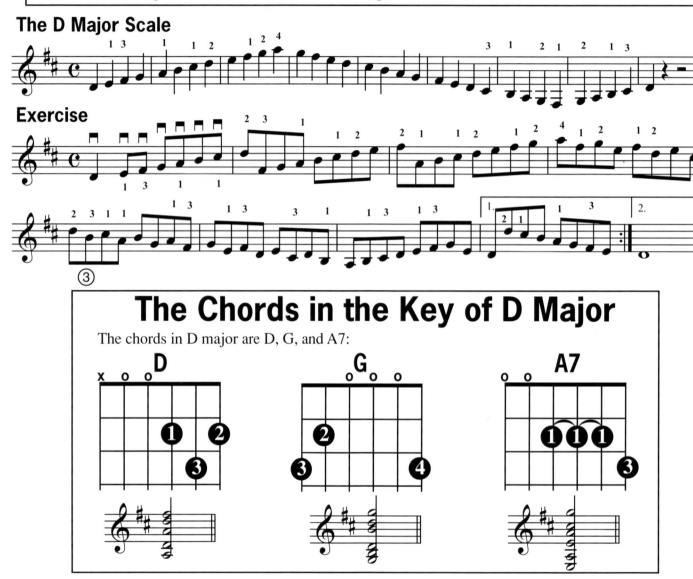

Exercise

The Chords in the Key of D Major

The chords in D major are D, G, and A7:

Accompaniment Styles

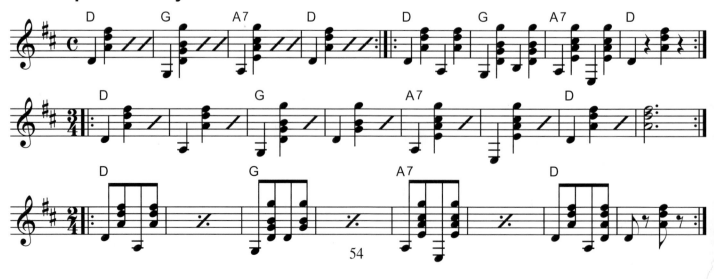

54

Key of D

Picking Studies

①

②

③

④

55

Rondo
Guitar Duet

CD 2 #18

M. Gebauer, Opus 10
Arr. by Mel Bay

Allegretto

Kirkwood Klucker

CD 2 #19

Swing Feeling

W. Bay

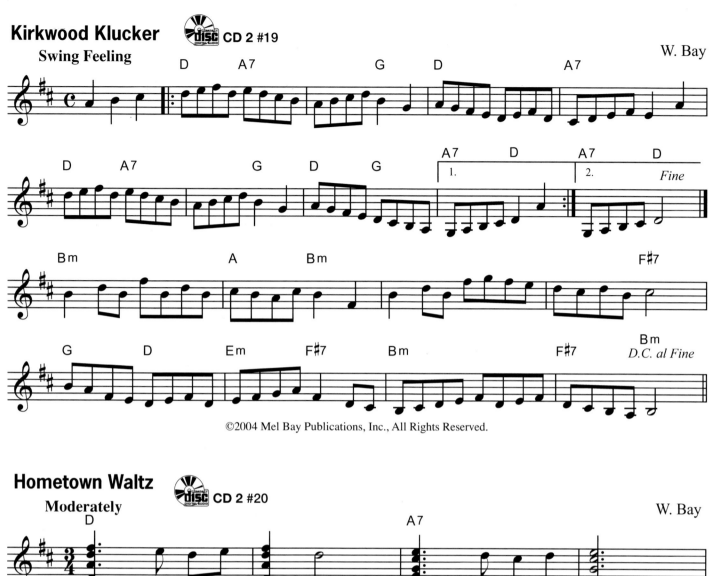

Hometown Waltz

CD 2 #20

Moderately

W. Bay

The D Scale in Two Octaves

Fingers 0 1 3 0 1 0 1 2 0 1 2 4 1 3 4

Frets 7 9 10

Exercise   CD 2 #21

Cielito Lindo
Guitar Solo
Allegretto   CD 2 #22

Arr. by Mel Bay

Second–Position Etude No. 1 CD 2 #23
(Key of D)

He's Got the Whole World in His Hands CD 2 #24
(Second Position)

The following selections will be played entirely in the second position. Please observe fingering.

Turkey in the Straw
(Second Position)   CD 2 #25

Soldier's Joy
(Second Position)   CD 2 #26

Cascades
(Second Position)

CD 2 #27

Moderately

W. Bay

D Boogie
(Second Position)

CD 2 #28

Etude
(Second Position)

CD 2 #29

W. Bay

©2005 Mel Bay Publications, Inc., All Rights Reserved.

Freefall
(Second Position)

CD 2 #30

W. Bay

©2005 Mel Bay Publications, Inc., All Rights Reserved.

Thirds in the Key of D

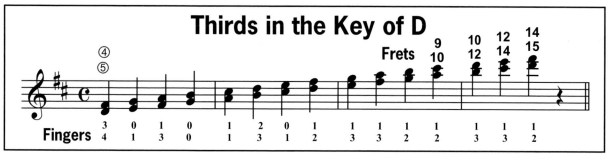

Drink to Me Only with Thine Eyes
Guitar Solo

CD 2 #31

Arr. by Mel Bay

Andante

Fine

D.C. al Fine

Caprice
Guitar Duet

CD 2 #32

Mazas, Opus 38
Arr. by Mel Bay

Allegretto

Sixteenth Notes

In common time, four sixteenth notes equal one qurter note.

They may be counted in this manner:

1-six-teenth-notes, 2-six-teenth-notes, 3-six-teenth-notes, 4-six-teenth-notes

Table of Notes and Rests

Whole Note	𝅝	A Whole Measure Rest
Half Notes		A Half Rest
Quarter Notes		A Quarter Rest
Eighth Notes		An Eighth Rest
Sixteenth Notes		A Sixteenth Rest

In the fifth and ninth measures of the following study, an eighth note is followed by two sixteenth notes.

They may be counted in this manner:

1   &   a   2   &   a   3   &   a   4   &   a

A Speed Study in D (Second Position) CD 2 #33

Allegro

Count: 1 six teenth note 2 six teenth notes ②

1 & a 2 six teenth notes

1 & a 2 six teenth notes

66

Brunswick Stew

CD 2 #34

Allegro

W. Bay

©2005 Mel Bay Publications, Inc., All Rights Reserved.

The Clock

CD 2 #35

W. Bay

©2005 Mel Bay Publications, Inc., All Rights Reserved.

Drowsy Maggie

Lively Tempo

CD 2 #36

Irish

Bennett's Reel

Allegro

CD 2 #37

Fiddle Tune

Minuet in D
Guitar Duet

CD 2 #38

Arr. by Mel Bay

The Key of B Minor

(Relative to D Major)

The B Minor Scales

70

Picking Studies

Voyage

CD 2 #43

W. Bay

Andante

©2005 Mel Bay Publications, Inc., All Rights Reserved.

Quiet Thoughts

CD 2 #44

W.Bay

Andante

©2005 Mel Bay Publications, Inc., All Rights Reserved.

The Chords in the Key of B Minor

The chords in the key of B minor are Bm, Em and F#7.

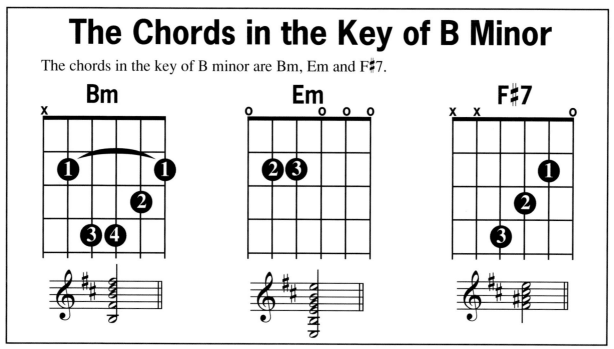

Accompaniment Styles

Waltz in B Minor

Guitar Solo   Andante   CD 2 #45

Duet in B Minor

Guitar Duet

CD 2 #46

Gebauer–Bay

5th Avenue Swing

Swing Feeling

CD 2 #47

W. Bay

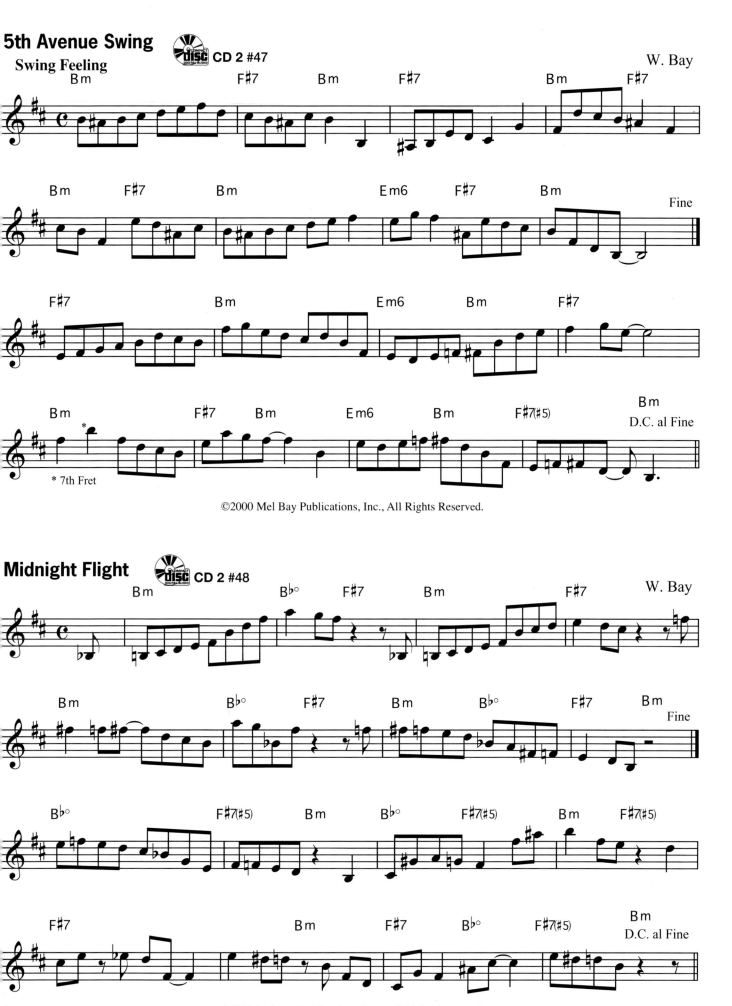

* 7th Fret

Midnight Flight

CD 2 #48

W. Bay

75

The Technical Names of the Chords

As we learned earlier, each degree of the scale has a technical name.

Chords built upon a scale degree will bear the technical name of that degree.

The three principal chords in any key are the **tonic, subdominant,** and the **dominant seventh**.

I   IV   V   Octave

Note that the chords are built upon the tonic, subdominant, and the dominant degrees of the scale.

The lowest tone of a chord is called the **root** and the remaining tones are numbered according to their distance from that root.

Six-Eight Time

This sign ![6/8 time signature] indicates **six-eight** time.

6 – beats per measure.
8 – type of note receiving one beat.

An eighth note ♪ = one beat, a quarter note ♩ = two beats, a dotted quarter note ♩. = three beats, and a sixteenth note ♬ = 1/2 beat.

Six-eight time consists of two units containing three beats each.

It will be counted: ♪♪♪ ♪♪♪ with the accents on beats one and four.
               1   2   3   **4**   5   6

The Irish Washerwomen

CD 2 #49

Arr. by Mel Bay

Guitar Solo   **Allegro**

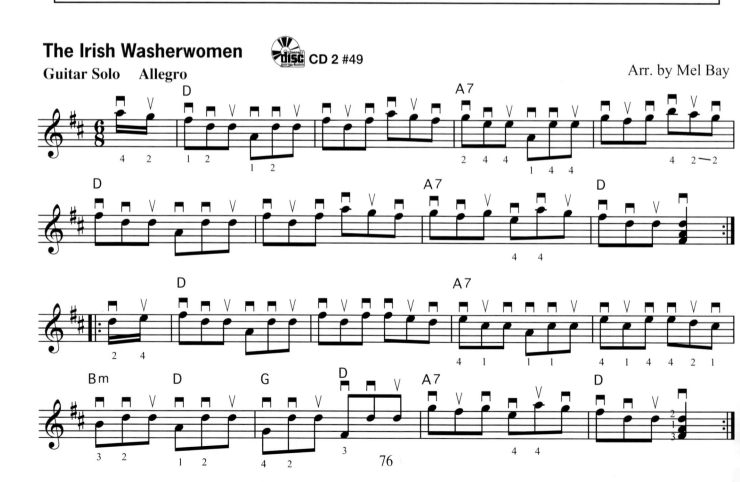

76

6/8 Picking Studies

⑤ CD 2 #52

⑥

⑦ CD 2 #53

⑧

⑨ CD 2 #54

Dublin Dance CD 2 #55

Lively

W. Bay

Fine

D.C. al Fine

Swallowtail Jig

CD 2 #56

Moderately

Irish Jig

Territory Ahead

CD 2 #57

Slowly

W. Bay

Minuet

Guitar Duet

CD 2 #58

J. S. Bach
Arr. by Mel Bay

Three-Eight Time

This sign $\begin{array}{c} 3 \\ 8 \end{array}$ indicates **three-eight** time.   3 – beats per measure.

8 – type of note receiving one beat.

An eighth note ♪ = one beat, a quarter note ♩ = two beats, a dotted quarter note ♩. = three beats, and a sixteenth note ♬ = 1/2 beat.

A Spanish Dance

CD 2 #59

Arr. by Mel Bay

Guitar Duet
Lively

A Spanish Dance (cont.)

83

Plectrum Technique

The following studies are excellent for the development of plectrum technique. Follow the stroking carefully and play slowly at first, increasing speed gradually.

Prelude CD 2 #60

Etude CD 2 #61

The Plectrum Waltz CD 2 #62

Carcassi - Bay

Skipping Along

Guitar Solo

CD 2 #63

Allegretto

Carcassi-Bay

Coronado

Guitar Solo

CD 2 #64

Carcassi-Bay

85

Dotted Eighth Note

A dotted eighth note is equal to

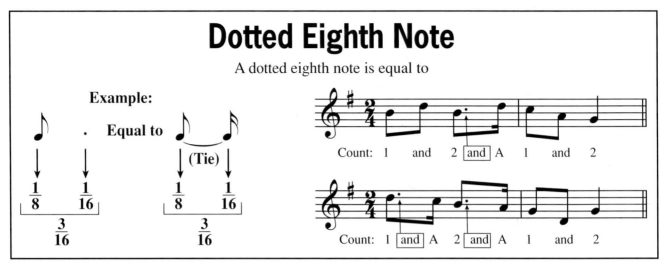

Country Gardens

Guitar Duet
Moderato

CD 2 #65

English Folk Dance
Arr. Mel Bay

ogan's Bluff CD 2 #66

Moderately

W. Bay

©1999 Mel Bay Publications, Inc., All Rights Reserved.

Blessed Quietness CD 2 #67

Slowly

Gospel Song

Harvest Moon Strathespy

Moderately

CD 2 #68

W. Bay

©1999 Mel Bay Publications, Inc., All Rights Reserved.

Alastair's Lament

Slow, march like tempo

CD 2 #69

W. Bay

©1999 Mel Bay Publications, Inc., All Rights Reserved.

Brighton Beach

Spirited tempo

CD 2 #70

W. Bay

©1999 Mel Bay Publications, Inc., All Rights Reserved.

Days of 'Lang Syne

CD 2 #71

Scottish